# NANCY MOORE

# WHO YOU ARE STAND BETWEEN YOU AND SUCCESS

*5 Tip On How To Identify Your Habit, Personal Capability, Trait, And Build Your Influential Personality*

# WHO YOU ARE STAND BETWEEN YOU AND SUCCESS

## 5 Tips On How To Identify Your Habit, Personal Capability, Trait, And Build Your Influential Personality

NANCY MOORE

# *Contents*

# *INTRODUCTION*

Knowing who you truly are is the beginning of important journey aspect of your life. Practically, many people have gone through live without knowing what they truly are. Presently, some people are living without self-knowledge. Invariably, knowing yourself stands between you and success.

In to the solo journey of finding yourself, it might appear as selfish objective but, it is very crucial for to everything you will go through in live. For instance, to be the most important person in the world, the best partner, parent, and so on, you must first understand who you are, what you value, and, ultimately, what you have to offer.

That is to say, every individual will benefit from taking this personal adventure. It's a process of breaking down and removing phases that don't serve you in your life or don't reflect who you truly are. However, it also entails a massive act of self-development, understanding who you want to be and pursuing your particular destiny, whatever that may be – with zeal.

Finding who you truly are is not something to be afraid of or avoid, but something to seek out with curiosity and compassion. This book, Who You Are Stand Between You And Success; 5 Tips On How To Identify Your Habit, Personal Capability, Trait, And Build Your Influential Personality, has identified Five tips which can be employed as a guideline on the journey of finding yourself.

I am an authority psychologist and motivational speaker. I have helped countless number of people globally in their solo journey of finding themselves. Therefore, the tips in this book have been prescribed and practiced by many people. People have been able to grasp what they truly are via these tips.

In the book, section I precisely, speaks briefly on how to define yourself. While section II speaks extensively on five tips on how to identify yourself. The tips like: Identifying Yourself; Developing Your Personal Brand; Develop Self-Awareness; Investigate Your Personality; Meeting Your Needs.

Evidently, you are the worst critic of yourself. To silence the inner critic, you have to read this book till the last page. Don't forget who you are stand between you and success. Thus, for you to be successful, you must know who you are.

## *Section I*

## *YOURSELF*

## *DEFINE WHO YOU ARE BY YOURSELF*

## *KNOW YOURSELF*

# *DEFINE YOURSELF*

Everyone is trying to figure out who they are at their core. When they define themselves, they frequently concentrate on the negative or how they compare to others. Nobody but you has the power to define who you are.

Identifying yourself is the beginning of the most crucial and life-changing endeavor of your life. Nevertheless, many people find it extremely difficult to define themselves. This could happen especially by listening to one's inner critic voice which destabilizes ones confidence of knowing who you are.

You mingle self-awareness with self-indulgence, and you continuing living without asking who you really are. Finding yourself may appear to be a purely selfish objective, yet it is actually a selfless process that underpins everything you do in life. To be the most important person in your world, the best partner, parent, and so on, you must first understand who you are, what you value, and, ultimately, what you have to offer.

# *Section II*

# *YOURSELF*

## *5 TIPS ON HOW TO IDENTIFY YOURSELF*

**Tip 1: Identifying Yourself**

**Tip 2: Developing Your Personal Brand**

**Tip 3: Develop Self-Awareness**

**Tip 4: Investigate Your Personality**

**Tip 5: Meeting Your Needs**

# *5 TIPS ON HOW TO IDENTIFY YOURSELF*

How will you be able to identify yourself? According to studies, the following are tips on how to identify and distinguish you.

**Tip #1: Identifying Yourself**

**1.**

Know who you are. Self-awareness, particularly nonjudgmental self-awareness, are crucial elements in helping you define yourself. Before you can identify who you are as a person, you must first grasp what makes you think and what your mental processes are.

Mindfulness entails paying attention to your thoughts and observing your mental patterns. You might notice, for example, that you have a propensity to believe that no one cares what you think and that your thoughts are meaningless. Recognizing that you experience these thoughts and capturing them before they cause you worry can help you put the pieces of your identity together.

You'll need to practice attentive non-judgment once you start paying attention to your mental processes and habits. This entails being aware of and accepting your mental patterns, but not berating yourself for them. Negative mental patterns and processes exist in everyone. You can get rid of them from your mind if you pay attention to them.

**2.**

Take note of how you refer to yourself. Look for the ways in which you identify yourself once you've started paying attention to how you think about yourself and the world. Examine the groups and communities with which you form your identity. All of these factors influence how you see yourself and reveal what you're allowing to define you.

Examine whether you describe yourself in terms of religion, nationality, or sexual identity, for example. Examine the roles you play in your life, such as your employment, your family (mother, father, sister, brother), and your love situation (single, couple, etc.).

**3.**

Make a list of your thoughts and self-definitions. Write down your thought processes and definitions as you identify them in a journal to become more skilled at identifying how they influence how you act and who you are. You'll be able to see how you think of yourself, making it easier to break negative associations.

Practically, speaking with or working with a clinical psychologist can greatly aid in the discovery of thought and behavior patterns. They can also assist you in dealing with the negative aspects of your mind.

## Tip 2: Developing Your Personal Brand

**1.**

Make a list of your negative definitions. You can let go of them by recording them and paying attention to them. Bringing them to the surface can help you loosen their grip on your mind and self.

Don't put oneself in a limiting situation. The action is determined by the self-definition. If you define yourself as someone who has had negative romantic relationships, for example, you've already ruled out the possibility of having a good love connection. It's a tale you tell yourself, and since you believe it, you'll already be acting in ways that prove the story to be real.

**2.**

Make a list of your basic values. Outside influences are dynamic and prone to constant change, therefore you don't want to define yourself solely on them. You will have a better chance of establishing a consistent self-definition if you base your self-definition on essential principles.

If you base your self-identity on qualities you hold dear, such as compassion, courage, and integrity, you will not lose it.

Make a list of these principles and act on them intentionally and mindfully in your daily life. As a result, if one of your core values is courage, speak up for someone who is being harassed at the bus stop, or if honesty is a fundamental value, admit that you have misplaced your father's favorite watch. Spend time volunteering at a homeless shelter if compassion is on your agenda.

**3.**

Make a positive self-definition. This is not to say that you are unaware of the unpleasant events and behaviors that have occurred in your life. They are just as much a part of you as the positive aspects, but they do not define who you are.

This means you should not let your identity be shaped by situations outside of your control. Those that come from the inside out, from the underlying principles you've previously established are essential to your identity.

Recognize that your terrible life events have taught you something. If you've had bad romantic encounters in the past, for example, learn from them. What have they taught you about the person you aspire to be?

***Warnings***

Don't try to compare yourself to others; you can't; it's not fair to them or to you; you have different origins, insecurities, and expectations of life and of yourself. Comparing two persons is like removing all of those things and putting them in a product comparison to determine which one is better.

***Personal Development Self Examination***

A true self-identification is a necessity step toward happiness and contentment. Determine the characteristics that distinguish you in order to discover your genuine self. Reflection and meditation on a daily basis might help you develop a better knowledge of your own identity. Overtime, you can build on your discoveries to form a crucial and meaningful relationship with yourself.

### *Tip 3: Develop Self-Awareness*

**1.**

Learn to be truthful to yourself. Knowing yourself entails identifying various aspects of your personality, identity, and existence. The idea is to perceive and accept all aspects of your personality rather than to criticizing yourself. Allow yourself to be open to the possibility of discovering new things about yourself.

Pay attention to various areas of your self-evaluation that make you uncomfortable. These emotional signals can reveal whether you're attempting to avoid a topic; are you self-conscious about that trait? If that's the case, what can you do about it?

Ask yourself why you don't like looking in the mirror, for example. Are you self-conscious about your appearance? Are you self-conscious about your age? Consider whether or not this is a fear you can overcome.

**2.**

Pose insightful questions to yourself. This understanding might assist you in determining what makes you happy or stressed. This information can assist you in spending more time on activities and goals that are beneficial to you. You could ask the following questions:

- What are your favorite pastimes?
- What are your life goals?
- What do you want to be remembered for?
- What do you consider to be your most serious setbacks?
- What are some of your blunders?

- What do others think of you?
- What do you want them to think about you?
- Who is your favorite role model?

**3.**

Listen to the voice inside your head. What you feel and believe is expressed through your inner voice. It responds when anything irritates or delights you. Make an effort to hear that inner voice. What is it trying to say? What does it think about the world around you?

Take a look in the mirror. Begin defining yourself, either aloud or silently in your brain. Are the descriptions favorable or unfavorable? Are they more interested in your appearance than your actions? Do you talk about your accomplishments or your setbacks?

Stop yourself from thinking badly and ask yourself why you are reacting the way you are. Shaming or condemning yourself could be an indication that you're trying to protect yourself from unwelcome ideas.

These thoughts, both positive and negative, shape how you see yourself. If your personal picture does not reflect who you want to be, you might consider taking measures to improve your personal qualities or develop new skills.

**4.**

Every day, keep a journal. Journaling allows you to become more aware of your motivations, feelings, and beliefs, allowing you to make more informed decisions in your life. Write down what you did, felt, and thought during the day for a few minutes each day. If you had a bad encounter, write down what happened and how it affected you. If you made a mistake, think about how you could improve.

In your writings, look for patterns. You may notice yourself repeating specific demands and desires over time. You are free to write anything comes to mind. Free writing might assist you in identifying what is upsetting you by allowing you to access your subconscious ideas.

Alternatively, you might utilize writing prompts to help you get started. Select prompts that require you to describe certain aspects of your personality or habits.

**5.**

Make mindfulness a part of your daily routine. Mindfulness is the practice of paying attention to the present moment in order to better understand one's own thoughts and behaviors. Mindfulness is often associated with daily meditation, but it also encompasses other techniques. Most significantly, it's a condition of being aware of yourself and the environment around you.

Check in with your five senses for a bit. What are you touching, smelling, hearing, and seeing? Every day, take a few minutes to simply pause and observe the world around you. Try to be aware of as many sensations as possible. What do you hear, feel, taste, and smell while you're alone? Question yourself when you have an emotional reaction. What makes you feel this way? What went wrong?

**6.**

Recognize your own body image. Make a list of adjectives that describe your appearance. After you've finished, go over this list again. Is this a list of bad or positive characteristics? Try to come up with strategies to love your body if you have a poor body image. Body confidence can translate to confidence in other areas of your life.

Make an effort to transform your negative thoughts into good ones. For example, if you're self-conscious about a mole, consider calling it a beauty mark. Keep in mind that many well-known actresses had beauty marks. Consider what you can do if something is actually making you miserable. If you're self-conscious about your acne, see a dermatologist or learn to wear cosmetics.

**Tip 4: Investigate Your Personality**

**1.**

Recognize the roles you play. Based on their personal relationships, career duties, and social contacts, everyone plays various parts in their lives. After you've outlined your responsibilities, think about what each one means to you. Underneath are some examples of roles:

- Parent
- Friend
- Leader of the group
- Emotional assistance
- Mentor/Mentee
- Confidante
- Creator

- Problem-solving expert

**2.**

Make a list of your **VITALS**. Values, interests, temperament, activities, life goals, and strengths are all abbreviated as VITALS. Try to define each of these categories for yourself in a notebook or word processor.

**Values**: What are the things that are most important to you? What qualities do you look for in yourself and others? What drives you to complete a task?

**Interests**: What kinds of things pique your interest? What do you enjoy doing in your spare time? What piques your interest? Make a list of ten adjectives that best represent your personality.

- What do you do for pastime during the day?

- What are your favorite aspects of your day?
- What are the least favorite aspect of your day?
- Do you have any routine that you follow on a daily basis?

**Goals in life:** What have been the defining moments in your life? Why? In five years, where do you see yourself? What will it be like in ten years?

What are your strengths in terms of abilities, skills, and talents? What do you excel at the most?

**3.**

Take a personality test on the internet. Personality tests aren't scientific, but they do pose questions that make you think about different parts of your personality. You can take a variety of respected examinations online. These are some of them:

- Meyers-Briggs Personality Type Indicator
- The Minnesota Multiphasic Personality Inventory is a questionnaire that assesses a person's personality (MMPI)
- Index Predictive Behavioral analysis
- The Big Five Personality Test

**4.**

Invite others to add their thoughts. While you should not define yourself based on what others say, soliciting feedback from others can help you understand aspects of yourself that you may not be aware of. Begin by asking family and friends to describe your personality or attributes.

If you're at ease, inquire about how your supervisor, mentor, or acquaintances perceive your personality. It's fine if you disagree with someone's observations! These remarks do not define you, and you may find that other people accept you more.

**5.**

Assess your level of satisfaction with your outcomes. Review what you learnt after you've assessed your personality and attributes to discover if you're satisfied with yourself. Do these characteristics and ideals reflect who you aspire to be? If you answered yes, think about how you can grow or strengthen these character characteristics. If the answer is no, make a list of personalized goals to work toward.

Make the most of your strengths to discover pleasure. For instance, if you've discovered that you're artistic and enjoy working with your hands, you might want to enroll in painting classes or begin a new hobby.

Use your knowledge of yourself to design a customized plan if you wish to improve something. You might learn to interact in small groups if you've learned you're introverted yet wish to become more social. You can have an interesting social life that works for you by balancing time alone with people.

**Tip 5: Meeting Your Needs**

**1.**

Self-care is important. It can be genuinely difficult to find time to reflect on yourself if you are overstressed with job. It's important to look after yourself emotionally and physically. Eventually, you'll feel at ease with who you are when you practice self-care. Self-care like:

- Make it a daily habit to exercise. You can either perform 20 minutes of exercise or go for a quick walk.
- Get 7-9 hours of sleep every night.
- Consume a nutritious diet consisting primarily of unprocessed fruits, vegetables, and whole grains.

- Make time to unwind every day. You can meditate or engage in a relaxing activity such as knitting, puzzles, or reading a book.

**2.**

Maintain a healthy work-life balance. Don't identify yourself entirely on the basis of your job title or advancement. While it is admirable to take pride in your profession, make time for yourself outside of it. It's in your best interest not to bring work home with you. Spend some time each day focusing on your other objectives, hobbies, and interests.

Work is vital, but you should also prioritize your personal well-being. Set work limits to ensure that work doesn't get in the way of your other relationships. Don't respond to non-urgent emails outside of business hours, for example.

**3.**

In your relationships, set boundaries. You will be happier in your relationships if you understand your limits. Identify the types of interactions that make you feel uneasy, agitated, or dissatisfied. These can be used to set personal limits.

Consider what kinds of situations make you uneasy. Do you, for example, despise crowds? Are there any jokes that make you uncomfortable? Think about someone in your life asks too much of you or forces you to do things you don't want to do. Determine which requests or expectations you are unable to fulfill.

**4.**

Make goals that will bring you joy. Setting goals will assist you in achieving your life's objectives. Make a list of a few goals that will assist you achieve your life goals. Aim for goals that will make you happy rather than ones that are motivated by extrinsic desires like money or prestige. For instance, you could set a target of writing 500 words every day. You should do this because you enjoy writing, not because you aspire to be a well-known author.

If you want, your goals can be simple and personal. Set a goal to enhance your cookie decorating talents by the holidays, for example. Set a few minor goals to help you get there along the way if you have a big aim. Set smaller goals to save money, acquire tickets, and plan your trip if your dream is to backpack across Europe.

**5.**

Review your wants and needs on a regular basis. Consider your life from time to time. Have any of your goals shifted? Is there something new in your life that's causing you to reevaluate your priorities? Self-awareness is a lifelong endeavor. Keep checking in on yourself like an old friend.

From time to time, read your literature and keep a notebook. This might assist you in determining how your habits or priorities have evolved over time. You may wish to re-evaluate how your habits, practices, and desires have altered after big life changes, such as a new job or a move.

You may want to let go of certain habits or tendencies if they no longer serve your needs or ambitions. Replace them with more productive activities that will aid in the achievement of your objectives.

# *Y.M.M.V*

(Your Mileage May Vary)

In Self Identification journey, feel free to take you can use, and leave the rest of tips.

Some tips might not work for you.

www.ingramcontent.com/pod-product-compliance
Lightning Source LLC
LaVergne TN
LVHW020531160826
845677LV00015B/4004